SCIENCEWORKS!

Be a Storm Chaser

By David Dreier

Storm Chaser Consultant: Warren Faidley

Series Consultant: Kirk A. Janowiak

Gareth Stevens
Publishing

Please visit our web site at www.garethstevens.com. For a free catalog describing our list of high-quality books, call 1-800-542-2595 (USA) or 1-800-387-3178 (Canada). Our fax: 1-877-542-2596

Library of Congress Cataloging-in-Publication Data available upon request from the publisher.
ISBN-13: 978-0-8368-8929-1 (lib. bdg.)
ISBN-10: 0-8368-8929-0 (lib. bdg.)
ISBN-13: 978-0-8368-8936-9 (softcover)
ISBN-10: 0-8368-8936-3 (softcover)

This North American edition first published in 2008 by
Gareth Stevens Publishing
A Weekly Reader® Company
1 Reader's Digest Road
Pleasantville, NY 10570-7000 USA

This U.S. edition copyright © 2008 by Gareth Stevens, Inc. Original edition copyright © 2007 by ticktock Media Ltd.
First published in Great Britain in 2007 by ticktock Media Ltd., Unit 2, Orchard Business Centre, North Farm Road,
Tunbridge Wells, Kent, TN2 3XF United Kingdom

ticktock Project Editor: Jo Hanks
ticktock Designer: Graham Rich
With thanks to: Sara Greasley

Gareth Stevens Editor: Jayne Keedle
Gareth Stevens Creative Director: Lisa Donovan
Gareth Stevens Senior Designer: Keith Plechaty

Printed in the United States of America

1 2 3 4 5 6 7 8 9 10 09 08 07

DAVID DREIER

David L. Dreier (B.S., journalism) is a freelance science writer. He spent much of his career at World Book Publishing in Chicago, Illinois, including six years as managing editor of *Science Year*, World Book's science and technology annual. He has also worked as a science reporter for a metropolitan daily newspaper, the San Antonio *Express-News*. In addition to writing about science, David has a great interest in history and has written a number of historical articles.

KIRK A. JANOWIAK

Kirk A. Janowiak (B.S. Biology & Natural Resources, M.S. Ecology & Animal Behavior, M.S. Science Education) has enjoyed teaching students from pre-school through college. He has been awarded the National Association of Biology Teachers' Outstanding Biology Teacher Award and was honored to be a finalist for the Presidential Award for Excellence in Math & Science Teaching. Kirk currently teaches Biology and Environmental Science and enjoys a wide range of interests from music to the art of roasting coffee.

WARREN FAIDLEY

Over the past 20 years, professional storm chaser Warren Faidley has photographed, written about, obsessed over, filmed, and somehow survived some of the planet's most breathtaking natural events. It is likely he has experienced more natural disasters than anyone—including baseball-sized hailstones, flash floods, lightning strikes, blizzards, earthquakes, firestorms, an F-5 tornado, and the interior of a category 5 hurricane. He was the first journalist, photographer, and cinematographer to make a successful professional career as a storm chaser.

CONTENTS

This book will help students develop these vital science skills:

- Abilities necessary to do scientific inquiry
- Understanding scientific inquiry
- Identifying properties of objects and materials
- Identifying position and motion of objects
- Understanding properties of earth materials
- Identifying objects in the sky
- Recognizing changes in earth and sky
- Abilities of technological design
- Understanding about science and technology
- Distinguishing between natural objects and objects made by humans
- Understanding personal health
- Characteristics and changes in populations
- Identifying types of resources
- Recognizing changes in environments
- Using science and technology in local challenges
- Understanding science as a human endeavor

Supports the National Science Education Standards (NSES) for Grades K–4

HOW TO USE THIS BOOK

Science is important in the lives of people everywhere. We use science at home and at school. In fact, we use science all the time. You need to know science to understand how the world works. Storm chasers need to understand the science of weather so they can track and record the most exciting storms. Scientists called meteorologists use this information to help protect us from life-threatening storms. With this book, you'll use science to chase storms.

This exciting science book is very easy to use. Check out what's inside!

INTRODUCTION

Do you have what it takes to be a storm chaser? Find out as you track and monitor storms.

FACTFILE

Read easy-to-understand information about how weather works.

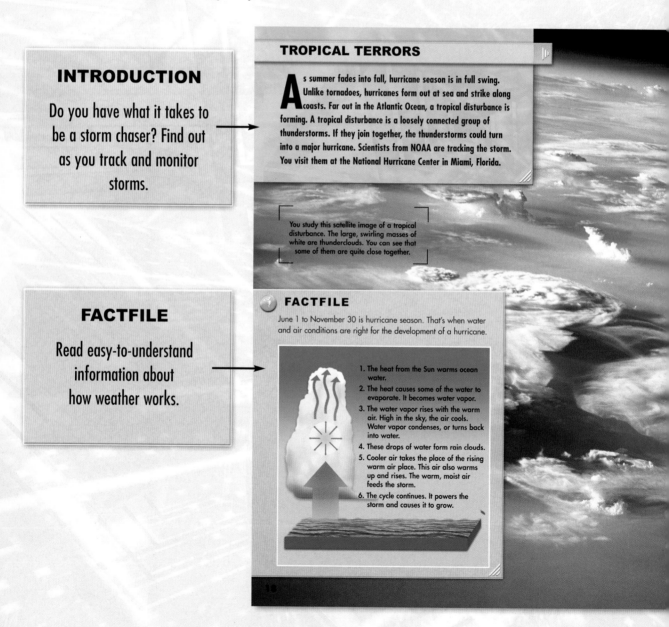

TROPICAL TERRORS

As summer fades into fall, hurricane season is in full swing. Unlike tornadoes, hurricanes form out at sea and strike along coasts. Far out in the Atlantic Ocean, a tropical disturbance is forming. A tropical disturbance is a loosely connected group of thunderstorms. If they join together, the thunderstorms could turn into a major hurricane. Scientists from NOAA are tracking the storm. You visit them at the National Hurricane Center in Miami, Florida.

You study this satellite image of a tropical disturbance. The large, swirling masses of white are thunderclouds. You can see that some of them are quite close together.

FACTFILE

June 1 to November 30 is hurricane season. That's when water and air conditions are right for the development of a hurricane.

1. The heat from the Sun warms ocean water.
2. The heat causes some of the water to evaporate. It becomes water vapor.
3. The water vapor rises with the warm air. High in the sky, the air cools. Water vapor condenses, or turns back into water.
4. These drops of water form rain clouds.
5. Cooler air takes the place of the rising warm air place. This air also warms up and rises. The warm, moist air feeds the storm.
6. The cycle continues. It powers the storm and causes it to grow.

WORKSTATION

Learn how storm chasers interpret weather data using diagrams, charts, graphs, and maps.

CHALLENGE QUESTIONS

Now that you understand the science, put it into practice.

IF YOU NEED HELP!

TIPS FOR SCIENCE SUCCESS

On page 30, you will find tips to help you with your science work.

ANSWERS

Turn to page 31 to check your answers. (*Try all the activities and questions before you take a look at the answers.*)

GLOSSARY

Turn to page 32 for definitions of storm chasing, weather, and science words.

WORKSTATION

The satellite readings at NOAA suggest a hurricane is on its way.

Satellites measure ocean surface temperatures, which must be at least 80° F (27° C) to make a hurricane. You find the following data for the Atlantic Basin. This area includes the North Atlantic Ocean, Caribbean Sea, and Gulf of Mexico.

	Water Temperature	Wind Speed	Atmospheric Conditions
North Atlantic Ocean	75° F	50 miles per hour (mph)	Partly cloudy skies
Caribbean Sea	79° F	15 mph	Thunderstorms
Gulf of Mexico	83° F	20 mph	Thunderstorms

Q CHALLENGE QUESTIONS

Before you can track a hurricane you need to study the NOAA readings.

1. Which of the three areas in the chart would be most likely to give birth to a hurricane? Why?
2. Which area would be least likely to produce a hurricane? Why?
3. What are the chances of a hurricane developing in the Atlantic Basin in February? Why?
4. Which of these water temperature readings shows the minimum temperature needed for hurricane development?

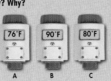

19

RACING TO A STORM

It's a hot June afternoon. You're driving across the Oklahoma plains. The television mounted in your van is tuned to a weather station. The forecaster is predicting a heavy storm season. As rain starts spattering the windshield, you turn on the wipers. Lightning bolts flash in the distance, and thunder rumbles. But you aren't concerned about finding shelter. You're a storm chaser. Racing to the scene of violent weather is what you do.

FACTFILE

- Most thunderstorms occur in spring and summer when it is warm. They can develop at any time of the year, however.

- A typical thunderstorm is about 15 miles (24 kilometers) wide. It lasts an average of 30 minutes.

Meteorologists measure air pressure to help them predict the weather.

- Air pressure is the force of air pressing down on Earth. Changes in air pressure give clues about the weather. High pressure usually means clear skies and cool weather. Low pressure can brings clouds and bad weather.

- Clouds form when warm, moist air rises. Warm air includes water vapor. High in the atmosphere, temperatures are colder. As the water vapor cools, it condenses, or changes into drops of water. These drops become rain clouds.

Cumulonimbus clouds can be more than 50,000 feet (15,240 meters) high. They can produce powerful storms.

Thunderstorms form when warm, moist air rises quickly, high into the atmosphere. There are several ways this can happen:

- **Left**: Warm land or sea heats the air above it. Warm air always rises. This transfer of heat is called convection.
- **Center**: Warm air is forced to rise as it moves over mountains.
- **Right**: When a mass of cold air collides with a mass of warm air, a front forms. The heavier cold air moves along the ground. The warm air is pushed upward.

 ## CHALLENGE QUESTIONS

1. What time of year do you chase most thunderstorms?
2. What type of weather does low pressure often bring?
3. How wide is a thunderstorm?
4. Where does the warm air go when a front is formed?

Y ou're driving through the heart of the storm. Every few seconds, a flash of lightning lights up the landscape. It is followed by a loud boom of thunder. Other vans are parked up ahead, and a TV crew is videotaping the storm. Meteorologists from the National Oceanic and Atmospheric Administration (NOAA) are here, too. Everyone is watching closely to see if the storm will produce a tornado. You pull over and join the other storm chasers to take pictures.

FACTFILE

Lightning is a flash of light that occurs when electricity moves between clouds or between clouds and the ground.

1. During a storm, strong air currents cause water droplets and ice particles to move around and bump into each other. The collisions create a charge of electricity.

2. Some particles become positively charged (+) and rise to the top of the storm cloud. Others become negatively charged (−). These particles cluster at the bottom of the cloud.

3. Opposite particles attract. The negative charges try to "leap" back to those with a positive charge. The leap causes an increase of electricity in the form of a giant spark—LIGHTNING!

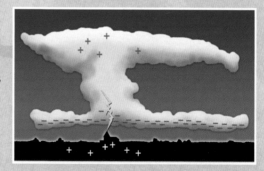

This artwork shows how negative particles in storm clouds are attracted to positive charges on the ground. The result is a bolt of lightning.

Storm chasing is risky. Heavy rain makes it hard for you to see. Flooded roadways make it hard for you to drive. Lightning can strike you.

- More than 500 people in the United States are injured by lightning each year. More than 100 people die.

- The average cloud-to-ground lightning bolt is about 3 miles (5 km) long. Some bolts travel in a straight line for more than 50 miles (80 km) before turning toward Earth.

- About 100 lightning flashes occur in storms around the world every second.

A lightning bolt heats the air around it to a temperature of about 55,000° Fahrenheit (30,538° Celsius). That's five times hotter than the surface of the Sun!

- If you could trap the energy in a typical lightning bolt, it could power a 100-watt light bulb for 90 days.

- The saying "Lightning never strikes twice in the same place" couldn't be more wrong. The Empire State Building in New York City was once struck by lightning 15 times in 15 minutes.

Q CHALLENGE QUESTIONS

1. How many times a second does lightning strike Earth's surface?

2. How many lightning bolts occur across the world in a minute? In an hour?

3. How does the science fact "opposites attract" apply to lightning?

4. Is it safe to stand in a spot where lightning just struck? Why or why not?

PREDICTING TORNADOES

S pring is usually the time of year for tornadoes, but twisters are hard to predict. Weather scientists use modern technology to help them pinpoint where and when a tornado is most likely to develop. To get the latest information, you visit the National Severe Storms Laboratory (NSSL) in Oklahoma. One of the NSSL scientists points to a radar picture on a computer screen. It has a color code. You can see a tornado is developing. If you hurry, you should be able to catch it in action!

FACTFILE

Radar is an important tool for spotting a growing tornado. A radar instrument sends out radio waves. The waves are reflected back by the storm. The reflected waves show the size and distance of the storm.

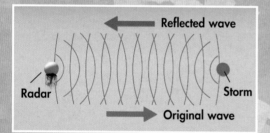

Radar   ← Reflected wave   Storm   → Original wave

Most meteorologists use Doppler radar. This type of radar tracks changes in weather systems. The NSSL's Doppler radar sends out several radio signals at once. It collects a lot of information about a storm in about a minute.

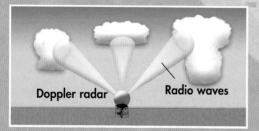

Doppler radar   Radio waves

+ ARCADIA

JONES +

+ SPENCER

NICOMA PARK +

MIDWEST CITY +

+ DEL CITY

TINKER
AIR FORCE BASE +

The sky here is clear of storm clouds.

A tornado is likely coming or has arrived in this area.

A severe thunderstorm warning has been sent to this area.

+ LUTHER

+ FOWLER

+ HARRAH

Flash floods have occurred or may occur in this area.

A warning comes through from the National Weather Service. The tornado is about to hit! You race to your truck.

TORNADO WARNING

THE NATIONAL WEATHER SERVICE IN DODGE CITY HAS ISSUED A TORNADO WARNING FOR...
JONES IN OKLAHOMA COUNTY UNTIL 3:00 PM.

AT 2:17 PM ... NATIONAL WEATHER SERVICE METEOROLOGISTS WERE TRACKING A LARGE AND EXTREMELY DANGEROUS TORNADO 14 MILES NORTHEAST OF DEL CITY ... MOVING NORTHEAST AT 25 MILES PER HOUR.

THIS IS AN EXTREMELY DANGEROUS AND LIFE-THREATENING SITUATION. IF YOU ARE IN THE PATH OF THIS TORNADO, TAKE COVER IMMEDIATELY.

GO TO A BASEMENT OR OTHER UNDERGROUND SHELTER AND GET UNDER SOMETHING STURDY.

A satellite image of a tornado

- Scientists at the NSSL are always developing better ways to predict tornadoes.
- In the early 1990s, the warning time for a tornado was about six minutes. Today, it's about 15 minutes. The extra time has helped save many lives.

Q CHALLENGE QUESTIONS

1. Look at the main radar image. Name the five cities that are now in danger from the tornado.
2. Look at the main radar image. Which city is in the most danger of flash floods?
3. What should you do if you are in the path of a tornado?
4. In which season do the most tornadoes occur?

SUPERCELLS AND TORNADOES

You race across the Oklahoma plains toward Jones, hoping to get there before the tornado hits. You're in the best place in the world for observing tornadoes. The plains of the central United States are known as Tornado Alley. Ahead you see a towering dark cloud. It's a supercell, a huge swirling storm that could become a twister!

FACTFILE

- Supercells are huge, rotating storms.
- They can produce heavy rains, severe lightning, and damaging hail.

Supercell

How a Supercell Forms

Supercells form when warm, moist air from the south meets cold, dry air from the north.

- Warm air rises over cold air in a circular motion. The air starts to rotate, or spin.

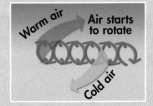

- An updraft (an upward air movement) twists the rotating air into a vertical column. The air starts to move faster. The rotating column of air at the center of the storm gets narrower. It stretches downward. A supercell has been formed.

- The rotating air in a supercell may then form a funnel-shaped cloud. If the funnel touches the ground, a tornado is born.

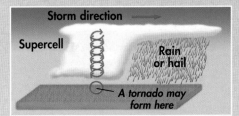

- The center of the funnel is called the vortex. It acts like a vacuum cleaner, sucking up warm air and dirt as it travels across the ground.

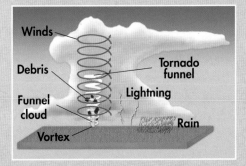

Q CHALLENGE QUESTIONS

Use the diagram above to answer these questions.

1. What is the center of a tornado's funnel called?
2. What makes the rotating air in supercells go vertical?
3. When does a supercell become a tornado?
4. What causes the air in supercells to begin to rotate?

CONFRONTING A TORNADO

You've arrived at the scene of the action. A huge supercell darkens the sky. A curtain of rain and hail hangs beneath it. Lightning bolts flash. You jump out of your van to take pictures. The storm gathers strength. Then comes the moment you've been waiting for: A huge whirling funnel descends from the clouds. It's only hundreds of feet away. It's a tornado! You watch as it tears an empty farmhouse from the ground and scatters the timbers like toothpicks. It's an awesome sight.

FACTFILE

Top: Sometimes a tornado has mini vortices circling around it or branching off from it. This is called a multiple vortex tornado. It can cause a great deal of damage.

Bottom: On average, tornadoes are 400 to 500 feet (122 to 152 m) wide. They travel about 4 miles (6 km) and last only a few minutes. A large tornado, however, can span a mile or more. It may last for more than an hour.

WORKSTATION

Where Tornadoes Occur

This map shows the areas of the world where tornadoes are mostly likely to occur.

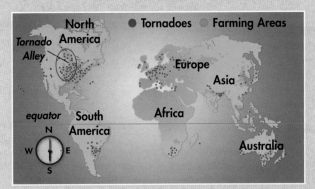

- Tornadoes often develop in farming areas.
- The United States has more than 1,000 tornadoes a year. That is the most of any country.
- Most tornadoes in the United States occur in Tornado Alley. This area of the Midwest has a lot of farms. In Tornado Alley, hot air traveling north from the Gulf of Mexico meets cool, dry air from Canada and the west. This creates large thunderclouds.
- Canada has the second highest number of tornadoes a year, about 100.
- The United Kingdom has more tornadoes per square mile than any other country. Fortunately most are weak.
- South of the equator, Australia has the most tornadoes.

Q CHALLENGE QUESTIONS

1. How wide is the average tornado?
2. What causes so many tornadoes to hit Tornado Alley?
3. Do most tornadoes happen above the equator or below it?
4. The number of tornadoes in the United States each year is how many times greater than the number in Canada?

AFTER THE TORNADO

You're back in your van, following the path of the tornado. You see smashed houses, uprooted trees, and wrecked cars. Even for a storm chaser, this has hardly been a typical day. It isn't often that you're able to witness such a powerful tornado. You're glad you got to see this one. Thanks to advance warning, this twister caused no deaths and only a few injuries. The work of meteorologists and storm chasers is helping to predict tornadoes and to save lives.

LOOK OUT!

Tornadoes can pick up things and throw them with great force. That is part of what makes them so dangerous. The tornado sent this fork flying into a tree. Fortunately, no one was in the fork's path!

The Enhanced Fujita (EF) Scale

Scientists use this scale to measure the strength of tornadoes.

Category: EF0   Wind speed: 65–85 mph*
Surfaces peeled off some roofs; damage to outside of houses; tree branches broken off.

Category: EF1   Wind speed: 86–110 mph
Roofs severely stripped; outer doors ripped away from houses; windows broken.

Category: EF2   Wind speed: 111–135 mph
Roofs torn off well-constructed houses; large trees uprooted; cars lifted off the ground.

Category: EF3   Wind speed: 136–165 mph
Entire sections of well-built houses destroyed; severe damage to large buildings; heavy vehicles lifted and thrown a short distance.

Category: EF4   Wind speed: 166–200 mph
Well-constructed houses completely destroyed.

mph = miles per hour

Category: EF5   Wind speed: 201+ mph
House foundations swept away; cars thrown more than 100 yards; even steel-reinforced buildings have significant structural damage.

Q CHALLENGE QUESTIONS

Use the Enhanced Fujita Scale to answer the questions below.

1. As you watch, the tornado tears the roof from a well-built house. What is the lowest category of tornado that could do this?

2. The tornado is getting worse. A car is hurled into the air. It must have been thrown 120 yards! What category is the tornado? What must the wind speed be?

3. The tornado had a wind speed of 166 miles per hour (mph). How much faster would the wind speed need to be for the tornado to become an EF5 tornado?

TROPICAL TERRORS

As summer fades into fall, hurricane season is in full swing. Unlike tornadoes, hurricanes form out at sea and strike along coasts. Far out in the Atlantic Ocean, a tropical disturbance is forming. A tropical disturbance is a loosely connected group of thunderstorms. If they join together, the thunderstorms could turn into a major hurricane. Scientists from NOAA are tracking the storm. You visit them at the National Hurricane Center in Miami, Florida.

You study this satellite image of a tropical disturbance. The large, swirling masses of white are thunderclouds. You can see that some of them are quite close together.

FACTFILE

June 1 to November 30 is hurricane season. That's when water and air conditions are right for the development of a hurricane.

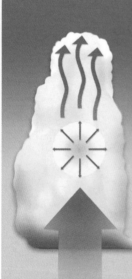

1. The heat from the Sun warms ocean water.
2. The heat causes some of the water to evaporate. It becomes water vapor.
3. The water vapor rises with the warm air. High in the sky, the air cools. Water vapor condenses, or turns back into water.
4. These drops of water form rain clouds.
5. Cooler air takes the place of the rising warm air place. This air also warms up and rises. The warm, moist air feeds the storm.
6. The cycle continues. It powers the storm and causes it to grow.

WORKSTATION

The satellite readings at NOAA suggest a hurricane is on its way.

Satellites measure ocean surface temperatures, which must be at least 80° F (27° C) to make a hurricane. You find the following data for the Atlantic Basin. This area includes the North Atlantic Ocean, Caribbean Sea, and Gulf of Mexico.

	Water Temperature	Wind Speed	Atmospheric Conditions
North Atlantic Ocean	75° F	50 miles per hour (mph)	Partly cloudy skies
Caribbean Sea	79° F	15 mph	Thunderstorms
Gulf of Mexico	83° F	20 mph	Thunderstorms

Q CHALLENGE QUESTIONS

Before you can track a hurricane you need to study the NOAA readings.

1. Which of the three areas in the chart would be most likely to give birth to a hurricane? Why?

2. Which area would be least likely to produce a hurricane? Why?

3. What are the chances of a hurricane developing in the Atlantic Basin in February? Why?

4. Which of these water temperature readings shows the minimum temperature needed for hurricane development?

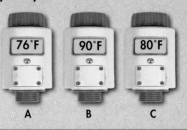

At the National Hurricane Center, you watch as the tropical disturbance becomes a tropical depression. You notice the towering rain clouds and strong winds. The storm is about 1,200 miles (1,931 km) east of Florida. It is moving toward the coast at about 35 miles (56 km) per hour. At that speed, it could reach land in less than 36 hours. You wonder if the storm will become a hurricane and hit Florida. The Hurricane Center has the data you need to predict how the storm will progress.

 FACTFILE

- Wind is created when air moves from a cool or cold area of high pressure to a warmer area of low pressure. In a tropical depression, air pressure is very low. So a lot of air moves in to the storm, creating fast-blowing winds.

- A tropical depression will only turn into a tropical storm or hurricane if the winds around it flow at a steady rate. If these winds flow at an uneven speed, or in different directions, the storm clouds will break up.

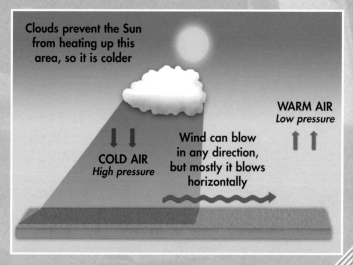

Clouds prevent the Sun from heating up this area, so it is colder

COLD AIR
High pressure

Wind can blow in any direction, but mostly it blows horizontally

WARM AIR
Low pressure

Here are the four stages that hurricanes go through to form. The stages are marked by changes in the storm's appearance and increasing wind speeds.

1. Tropical disturbance

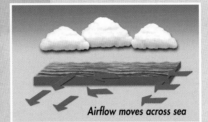

Airflow moves across sea

- Wind speed of 30 mph or less
- Scattered storms in one large area

2. Tropical depression

Airflow starts to flow inward

- Wind speed of 31–38 mph
- Large circling cloud mass

3. Tropical storm

Air starts to flow in circular motion

- Wind speed of 39–73 mph
- Large rotating storm without a center called the eye

4. Hurricane

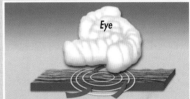

Eye

Air flows in increasingly tighter circular motion

- Wind speed of 74 mph and up
- Huge spiraling storm with a well-defined eye

Q CHALLENGE QUESTIONS

1. The winds in a tropical depression were blowing at 32 miles per hour (mph). They have increased by 5 mph. What type of storm is it now?
2. How many miles per hour does a storm have to reach before it is a hurricane?
3. If the winds around a tropical depression are blowing unevenly, what will happen to the storm?
4. You see these four satellite images. Name which stage of development each of these storms has reached.

A

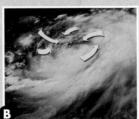

B

C

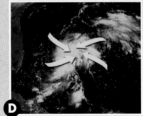

D

THE HURRICANE HUNTERS

By the next day, the Atlantic storm has become a full-fledged hurricane. It's now just 700 miles (1,127 km) from the coast. You are flying into the eye, or center, of a hurricane with members of the NOAA Hurricane Hunters. Suddenly you're surrounded by the swirling clouds of the mighty hurricane. Over the next few hours, you and the crew will use the plane's radar and weather instruments to measure the storm. Hold on, it's going to be a bumpy ride!

FACTFILE

- Satellite photos show only the size and shape of a hurricane.

- Hurricane Hunters use an instrument called a dropsonde to collect data. It records information about wind speed, temperature, and air pressure.

- This small weather-sensing canister is attached to a parachute. The dropsonde is dropped from the airplane. It travels through the hurricane and sends data back to the plane.

- The data is sent to the National Hurricane Center. There it is used to predict the strength and path of the hurricane.

These planes are above the hurricane's eye wall.

Inside a Hurricane

- The eye, or center, of a hurricane is 10 to 40 miles (16 to 64 km) wide. The eye has little wind and few clouds.
- The eye wall is a ring of thunderstorms around the eye. It has the strongest wind and the most rainfall in a hurricane.
- Two of the most important measurements in a hurricane are wind speed and air pressure. Hurricanes with the lowest air pressure in the eye usually have the strongest winds.

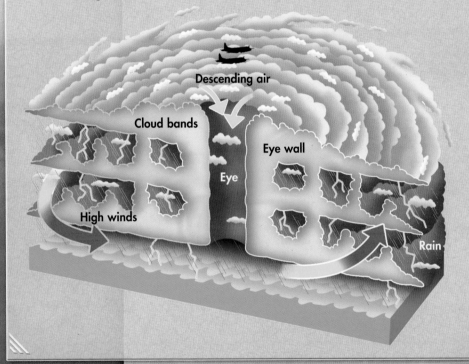

Descending air

Cloud bands

Eye wall

Eye

High winds

Rain

Q CHALLENGE QUESTIONS

1. Why aren't satellites alone used to collect information about hurricanes?
2. Which area of a hurricane has the strongest wind?
3. Which kinds of hurricanes have the strongest winds?
4. Where is the eye of the hurricane in the main photo on these pages?

EMERGENCY EVACUATION

The Atlantic storm has strengthened dramatically. It's now a Category 5 hurricane. That's the strongest kind, and it's headed for Miami. The huge storm is due to hit in about 12 hours. People are boarding up their windows and leaving. You join up with an Air Force rescue worker to help people who are trying to get away from the hurricane. The streets are full of cars heading out of town.

FACTFILE

A hurricane wouldn't gain such strength without the spin created by the rotation of Earth.

- In the Northern Hemisphere, winds blow counterclockwise.

- In the Southern Hemisphere, winds rotate clockwise.

- This swerve in winds caused by Earth's rotation is called the Coriolis effect.

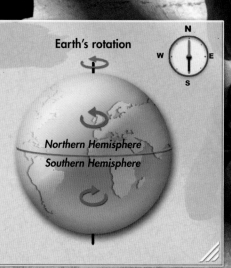

Earth's rotation

Northern Hemisphere
Southern Hemisphere

WORKSTATION

The Saffir-Simpson Hurricane Scale

Scientists use this scale to rate hurricanes. The categories are based on hurricane wind speed in miles per hour (mph). The scale also lists typical damage caused by each category of hurricane.

Category	Wind Speeds	Damage Caused
1	74 to 95 mph	Unanchored objects damaged or blown over
2	96 to 110 mph	Some smaller trees blown down; some damage to roofs and windows
3	111 to 130 mph	Some large trees blown down; some damage to houses and small buildings
4	131 to 155 mph	Many house roofs ripped off; complete destruction of mobile homes
5	156+ mph	Many houses and buildings severely damaged or destroyed

Q CHALLENGE QUESTIONS

1. In which direction does wind blow in the Northern Hemisphere?
2. Look at the chart above. How much wind speed would the most severe Category 1 hurricane have to gain to become a Category 4 hurricane?
3. When the storm you have been tracking was off the coast of Florida, it was a Category 5 hurricane. Its winds were clocked at 175 mph. When it hit land, the speed of its winds dropped to 125 mph. What category hurricane was it then?
4. After a hurricane, you visit a city that was hit. The damage does not appear to be too bad. You don't see any damage to buildings. No trees have fallen down. A lot of garbage cans have been knocked over, and you see some patio furniture in the street. What category was the hurricane?

BLASTED BY A HURRICANE

The hurricane is now beating the city with incredible fury. A heavy rain is falling, and the wind is blowing 170 miles (274 km) per hour. From your hotel room, you watch as windows blow in and roofs are ripped off buildings. Trees are flying down the street. Four hours later, the storm "calms down" and you go outside. The wind is still violent at 100 miles (161 km) per hour. You're thrown to the ground a few times. Toward the coast, the water gets deeper and deeper. Soon it is calf-high. None of this scares you. Firsthand pictures of a Category 5 hurricane are rare, and you want to record the storm for history.

FACTFILE

A storm surge is water pushed onto land by a hurricane. A storm surge is often a hurricane's most dangerous effect.

- A major hurricane can produce a storm surge more than 15 feet (4.5 meters) high.

- The storm surges of Category 5 hurricanes have often exceeded 20 feet (6 m).

A hurricane whips up seawater.

The hurricane moves toward land. Its strong winds push waves with it.

Flooding occurs on land. It causes more damage than wind does.

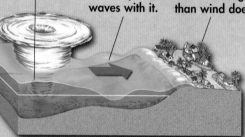

Storm surge

- The biggest storm surge ever recorded struck Australia in 1899. The surge was at least 42 feet (13 m) high. After the storm, people in the area reported finding fish and dolphins that had been thrown on top of 50-foot (15-m) cliffs.

WORKSTATION

As an experienced storm chaser, you are prepared for life-threatening situations. You make sure that you have everything on this list:

During a hurricane, shops and restaurants close down. Water supplies are often cut off. So you pack bottled water and high-energy foods.

 Power outages are likely. You take batteries, a flashlight, and candles.

You might need to drive away from the storm quickly! You carry extra gasoline, a basic car repair kit, a spare tire, and a road flare.

 If you get hurt, you have to take care of yourself. You carry a first aid kit.

You can't walk into the storm without any protection. You pack safety glasses, a rope, a water-resistant rescue strobe, and a life jacket.

 Finally, you pack the equipment you need to do your job. You need waterproof camera equipment and a handheld anemometer, a device that measures wind speed.

Q CHALLENGE QUESTIONS

1. What element of a hurricane often causes the most damage?
2. The hurricane knocked out the power in your hotel room. What items from the list should help you most?
3. Which piece of safety equipment will protect you from flying objects?
4. What device do you use to measure wind speed?

27

HURRICANE CHASE

You travel all over the world studying hurricanes. Some of them have lasted for seven days! The hurricane you have just experienced lasted about a day before moving on. The storm is not over yet, however. Thick clouds of heavy rain rolled in after the hurricane passed through. They are still causing flooding. You know the conditions in which hurricanes form. This knowledge may lead you to an area where another one is forming. Not even the experts at NOAA, however, can predict exactly when a hurricane will occur.

FACTFILE

Once a hurricane reaches land, it starts to weaken almost immediately. The main reasons for this are:

- It no longer has its energy source of warm, moist seawater.
- Contact with land disrupts its airflow. When that happens, the hurricane's eye fills with clouds, and it dies out.

A hurricane threw this car into a swimming pool.

WORKSTATION

The world's hurricane zones sit along the Tropics of Cancer and Capricorn. These are the northernmost and southernmost points on Earth where the Sun can be straight overhead.

- Hurricanes usually travel west. Then they turn away from the equator.
- If they begin beneath the equator, they move south toward the Tropic of Capricorn.
- If they begin above the equator, they move north.
- As they move, hurricanes pick up speed due to the Coriolis effect.

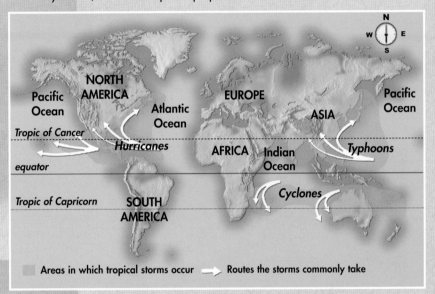

Areas in which tropical storms occur → Routes the storms commonly take

Hurricanes have different names in different parts of the world.

- When they occur in the Indian Ocean, they are tropical cyclones.
- When they occur in the Atlantic Basin or the northeast and southeast Pacific Ocean, they are hurricanes.
- When they occur in the western Pacific, they are typhoons.

Q CHALLENGE QUESTIONS

1. What causes a hurricane to die out?
2. A typhoon is forming between the equator and the Tropic of Cancer. Will it move north or south?
3. Tomorrow you are off to study a storm in the western Pacific. Will it be called a hurricane, a tropical cyclone, or a typhoon?
4. Would a storm chaser go to the United States to see a tropical cyclone? Why?

TIPS FOR SCIENCE SUCCESS

Pages 8–9

At the Center of a Thunderstorm

Remember that there are 60 seconds in a minute and 60 minutes in an hour. So if you know, for instance, how many times lightning strikes in a second, and want the amount for one minute, multiply it by 60. To get the amount for an hour, you can multiply that amount by another 60 or you can multiply the original amount by 3,600 (60 X 60).

Pages 16–17

After the Tornado

Experts estimate the wind speed of a tornado after the tornado is over by examining the damage it has caused. For example, if houses hit by a tornado have suffered only minor roof damage, you can conclude that the tornado was probably an EF0.

Pages 18–19

Tropical Terrors

Tornadoes and hurricanes differ in a number of ways. Tornadoes usually form far inland. Hurricanes form over warm ocean water and strike along coasts. Tornadoes form quickly and often last for only a few minutes. Hurricanes can take days to form and may last more than a week. Hurricanes are also much bigger than tornadoes. The biggest hurricanes can be 300 miles (483 km) wide. Yet tornado winds can be much faster than those in hurricanes. A tornado's winds can spiral up to 300 miles (483 km) miles per hour.

Pages 20–21

Birth of a Hurricane

It can be hard to tell the different stages of a storm using satellite images. Remember that a tropical depression is an air mass that has just begun to circle. Look for the satellite image in which the clouds have a slightly curved shape.

Pages 24–25

Emergency Evacuation

Air is a form of matter, just like water or sand. That is why we can feel air when it blows and why it exerts force on things. The faster air moves, the more force it exerts.

Earth is divided into a Northern Hemisphere and a Southern Hemisphere by an imaginary line called the equator.

ANSWERS

Pages 6–7

1. Spring and summer
2. Bad weather
3. 15 miles (24 km)
4. Warm air rises and cools to form clouds, which produce thunderstorms.

Pages 8–9

1. 100 times per second
2. 6,000 a minute; 360,000 an hour
3. A storm cloud has positive and negative charges. These opposite charges attract. If the negative charges become overcrowded, they "leap" to positive charges in the cloud or on the ground. This sudden leap creates lightning.
4. It is not safe. The saying "lightning never strikes twice in the same place" is not true.

Pages 10–11

1. Spencer, Nicoma Park, Midwest City, Del City, Jones
2. Arcadia
3. Take cover in a basement or other underground shelter.
4. Spring

Pages 12–13

1. Vortex
2. Updraft
3. When it forms a rotating funnel cloud that extends down to the ground
4. Warm air rises over cold air to create a circular motion.

Pages 14–15

1. 400 to 500 feet (122 to 152 km)
2. Hot air from the Gulf of Mexico meets cold air from Canada and the west. This creates thunderclouds that develop into tornadoes.
3. Above
4. 10 times greater

Pages 16–17

1. EF2
2. EF5; more than 200 mph
3. 35 mph or more

Pages 18–19

1. The Gulf of Mexico, because the water temperature is more than 80° F, and thunderstorms are occurring.
2. The North Atlantic Ocean, because the water temperature is less than 80° F, and there are few clouds.
3. Hurricanes are less likely to occur in February. Hurricane season runs from June until November.
4. C: 80° F (27° C)

Pages 20–21

1. The storm is still a tropical depression. It would not become a tropical storm until its wind speed reached 39 mph.
2. 74 mph
3. The storm clouds will break up. The storm will not grow into a tropical storm or a hurricane.
4. A: Hurricane; B: Tropical storm; C: Tropical disturbance; D: Tropical depression

Pages 22–23

1. Satellite photographs show only the size and shape of a hurricane.
2. Eye wall
3. Those with lowest air pressure in the eye
4. The eye is circled in this photo:

Pages 24–25

1. Counterclockwise
2. 36 mph (131 mph minus 95 mph)
3. Category 3
4. Category 1

Pages 26–27

1. Storm surge
2. Flashlight, batteries, and candles
3. Safety glasses
4. Handheld anemometer

Pages 28–29

1. Loss of contact with seawater, its main energy source; and contact with land
2. North
3. Typhoon
4. No, a storm chaser would not go to the United States to see a tropical cyclone. Tropical cyclones occur in the Indian Ocean.

AIR PRESSURE a force created by the weight of air pressing down on Earth's surface. Air pressure is low in the center of both hurricanes and tornadoes.

ATMOSPHERE the thick layer of air that surrounds Earth

CUMULONIMBUS CLOUD a towering thundercloud with a wide, flattened top

CONVECTION the transfer of heat that occurs when a liquid or gas moves

CORIOLIS EFFECT the curving motion of wind caused by Earth's rotation

DOPPLER RADAR a type of radar that can detect the motion of air in a storm

DROPSONDE a small weather-sensing canister attached to a parachute that is dropped into a hurricane to take measurements

EYE the relatively calm and cloudless center of a hurricane

EYE WALL circling tower of violent thunderstorms around the eye of a hurricane; it is where a hurricane's winds are fastest

FRONT the boundary where two air masses meet

METEOROLOGIST a scientist who studies Earth's weather and climate

RADAR an instrument that sends out radio waves and detects waves that are reflected by objects or storms

STORM SURGE a huge wall of water pushed inland by the powerful winds of a hurricane

SUPERCELLS large rotating thunderstorms that often produce tornadoes

TORNADO ALLEY a large area of plains in the Midwest where many tornadoes occur

TYPHOON the name for hurricane-type storm that occurs in the western Pacific Ocean

TROPICAL CYCLONE the name for a hurricane-type storm that occurs in the Indian Ocean

TROPICAL DEPRESSION a mass of thunderstorms with circling winds

TROPICAL DISTURBANCE a group of thunderstorms in one part of the ocean

TROPICAL STORM a large rotating storm system with winds that are not yet strong enough to make it a hurricane

PICTURE CREDITS

(b = below or bottom; c = center; f = far; l = left; r = right; t = top)

Getty: 6–7 (main), 8–9 (main), 12–13 (main), 12cl, 14–15 (main), 14b, 18–19 (main), 20–21 (main), 26–27 (main), 28–29 (main). **Oxford Scientific:** 17cr, 19c, 30br. **NASA:** 22cl. **National Oceanic and Atmospheric Administration/Department of Commerce:** 10–11 (main), 21bl, 21bcl, 21bcr, 21br, 22–23 (main), 30bl, 31bl. **Shutterstock:** 17tl Marek Slusarczyk, 17tr Robert A. Mansker, 17cl Laura Clay Ballard, 17bl William J. Mahnken, 17br, 27tr Piotr Przeszlo/ PhotoCreate / Magda Zurawska, 27tl Jeremy Smith/OPIS, 27br Michelle Marsan, 27bl Marek Slusarczyk/ Daniela Schrami, 27cr William Milner/Arvind Balaraman, 27cl ASP, 30tl. **ticktock media archive:** 7cl, 7cc, 7cr, 8br, 10c, 10b, 13t, 13ac, 13bc, 13b, 15t, 18b, 19c, 19b, 20b, 21tl, 21tr, 21cl, 21cr, 24b, 25c, 26bc, 29c, 23tc, 15c, 30tr. **U.S. Air Force photo by Master Sgt. Efrain Gonzalez:** 24–25 (main). **Weatherstock:** title page, 9c, 14bc, 16–17 (main), 17cl, 28b. **Weekly Reader:** 23r. **Wikimedia:** 7t.

Every effort has been made to trace the copyright holders, and we apologize in advance for any unintentional omissions. We would be pleased to insert the appropriate acknowledgments in any subsequent edition of this publication.